The Diabolo Book
Spinning a Top on a String with Hand Sticks

Jack Wiley

For more information about the author, go to: **http://www.amazon.com/author/jackwileypublications.**

ISBN-13: 978-1508663232
ISBN-10: 1508663238

CONTENTS

1   INTRODUCTION TO THE DIABOLO   5

2   DIABOLO MECHANICS   9
        Balance and Spinning—Gyroscopic Balancing

3   EQUIPMENT AND WORKOUT AREAS   12
        Diabolos—What to Wear—Workout Areas

4   INDIVIDUAL SKILLS   14
        Basic Spinning—Toss and Catch—Rock—Uphill Climb—
        Around the World—The Whip—Kangaroo Hop—String
        Bounce—Bounce Back—Foot Jump—One-Handed Spinning—
        One-Handed Toss—Stick Spin—Arm Crossing—Jumping
        Over Top—Cross Stick Catch and Toss—Loop—Double
        Loop—String Climb—The Circle Crisscross Toss and Catch

5   PARTNER AND GROUP SKILLS   27
        Cross String Pass—Toss and Catch Pass

6   COMPETITION AND GAMES   29
        Tournaments—Court Diabolo

        ABOUT THE AUTHOR   31

Chapter 1

INTRODUCTION TO THE DIABOLO

The "diabolo" is a top that is spun and controlled on a string attached to two sticks held by the operator. Diabolos are of many different shapes and sizes.

The diabolo is believed to have originated in China, where it is known as "Kouegen." This was a humming top made of two hollow bamboo cylinders joined by a short rod. Each cylinder was pierced with holes, which made a noise when the top was spinning.

According to one source, the diabolo was brought to England about 1794 by Lord Macartney. However, another source mentions that King Edward IV used a diabolo in England about 1470.

By 1812, the device was popular in France, where it was known as "le diable" or the devil. The term "diabolo" seems to have originated about this time, perhaps from the Greek "diaballo," which means "to throw." The term may have also derived from its

Typical diabolo shapes.

An 1812 French print of a young woman, aided by a male companion, learning to spin a diabolo.

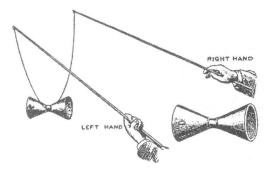

The flying cone version of the diabolo was popular in France in 1812.

having two balls joined together, with "dia" for "two" and "bolo" for "ball." It should be noted that "diablo" rather than "diabolo" means "devil" in Spanish.

The diabolo has also been called the "diavolo" and "the devil on two sticks." In 1812, there were a number of organizations organized for diabolo players, including Le Devil Club, Club du Jeu de Diable, Le Rochette, and Le Diabolo Club. These names suggest that the diabolo was known by several different names.

In 1812, the diabolo was not limited to children. In fact, most of the illustrations from this time show adults performing diabolo skills. Ladies and persons of great eminence are known to have enjoyed this activity.

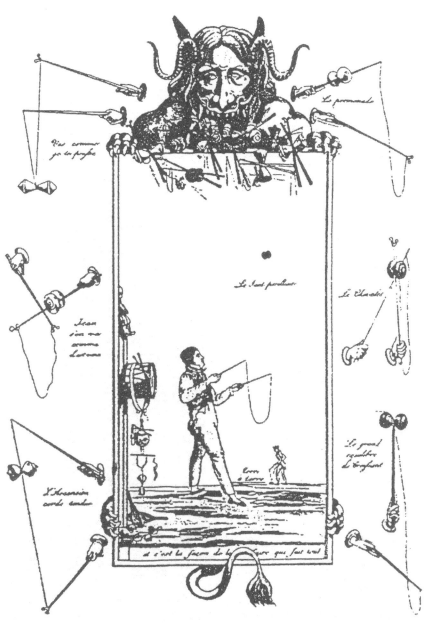

French drawing showing diabolo skills.

Drawing of diabolo players in France.

The French engineer, Gustave Phillipart, is reported to have improved the design of the diabolo in the early 1900s, and it became a popular sensation again in both France and England.

The first introduction in the United States is not known, but Parker Brothers introduced a manufactured version about 1907.

Like the yo-yo, the diabolo has enjoyed a number of surges in popularity in this country. Diabolo manufacturers have at various times sponsored diabolo competition in a manner similar to yo-yo competition.

The diabolo has been used in a number of different ways, the most popular of which is as a novelty skill toy for youngsters. The diabolo has also been used for competition. Various diabolo games have also been devised and played. The diabolo is also a popular performing device, especially in China.

Chapter 2

DIABOLO MECHANICS

The fascinating thing about diabolos and other tops is that they balance themselves while spinning. This ability of a spinning top to hold its position in space has long intrigued the imagination. Like all moving objects, a spinning top resists any attempt to change the direction of its motion. A convincing demonstration of this is to hold the front wheel of a bicycle by the axle with your fingers. Then use the thumbs or fingers to start the wheel spinning rapidly. Hold the spinning wheel with your arms extended in front of you. Then try to tilt the wheel or rotate the axle.

The faster the bicycle wheel is turning, the more it will resist change. Try different spinning speeds.

BALANCE AND SPINNING

Diabolo spinning is a combination of balance and spinning, since the diabolo top is spun on a string. The diabolo, regardless of whether it is stationary or spinning, has a center of gravity. This is a point where the entire weight of the top appears to be centered. The center of gravity of the diabolo, assuming it is accurately constructed, is in the exact horizontal and vertical center of the axle.

When a diabolo that is not spinning is placed on the diabolo string (supported by two hand sticks), the diabolo will not remain balanced on a tight string, since the center of gravity of the diabolo is above the string. The top tilts toward one end or the other and falls from the string.

Balance can be maintained if the string is moved so that the string remains directly under the center of gravity or is moving under the center of gravity more rapidly than the top is falling off balance.

GYROSCOPIC BALANCING

Spinning diabolo tops remains balanced on top of the string under certain conditions even though the center of gravity is above the string. This is called "gyroscopic balancing."

The spinning top resists any attempt to change the direction of its motion. A spinning top keeps on spinning at the same speed (revolutions per second) until an outside force slows it down, stops it, or speeds it up. This is the most important principle to keep in mind for understanding the mechanics of diabolo spinning.

How much the spinning diabolo resists change depends on how fast it is turning, how much it weighs, and how much of its weight is at the outer edge where the spin is fastest.

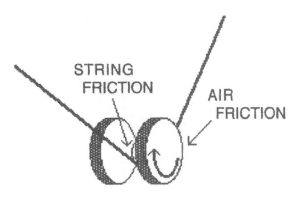

The spinning diabolo slows down because of friction of the top rubbing the string and air rubbing against the top as it spins.

The string is used to correct diabolo tilt.

The diabolo slows down because of friction of the top rubbing the string and air rubbing against the top as it spins.

Unless something else pulls it, the axis of a spinning diabolo keeps pointing in the same direction. In order to change the orientation of the string in relation to the spinning top, the string must be moved and/or a force must be applied to the diabolo (you must give the diabolo a push or pull).

The two major aspects of performing with a diabolo are (1) spinning the diabolo and (2) controlling the spinning diabolo.

The string is used both to spin and control the diabolo. Basic spinning is accomplished by pulling up quickly with the right hand, while lowering the left hand at the same time, as shown. The hands are returned gently to the starting position, allowing the string to slip past the spinning diabolo. This action is repeated with an easy rhythm. Actual techniques are covered in later chapters.

The string is also used to control the diabolo. For example, if the diabolo tip tilts

Basic spinning is accomplished by allowing string to turn diabolo in one direction and slip past diabolo in the other.

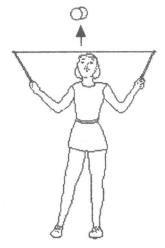

Tossing diabolo into air by pulling sticks rapidly apart.

toward you while you are doing the spinning action detailed above, pushing the right hand stick away from you will move the diabolo upright again. If the diabolo tip tilts away from you, pulling the right hand stick toward you will move the diabolo to an upright position. Control techniques for performing diabolo skills are covered in later chapters.

Another important mechanic is tossing the spinning diabolo into the air. This can be accomplished by spinning the diabolo on a slack string and moving the sticks outward rapidly. This action is used for performing a variety of diabolo skills.

Chapter 3

EQUIPMENT AND WORKOUT AREAS

Many different shapes, sizes, and weights of diabolos have been tried, and these have been constructed from a variety of materials. I have a large collection of diabolos, and some of them work much better than others. What are the best shape, size, and weight? This has long been a subject of debate, and new designs are still being tried. Most of the popular diabolos that are presently being manufactured work well. Most of the popular diabolos that are presently being manufactured work well. Many designs are available from Amazon: **http://www.amazon.com/ diabolos/.**

My own personal preference is the design shown below that is available from Brian Dube: **http://www.dube.com/diabolo/.** This diabolo has all rubber ends and a machined aluminum center. It comes complete with hand sticks and string.

The hand sticks and string are an important part of performing with a diabolo. Various types and lengths of string are used, and these can be attached to the hand sticks in various ways, but are usually either attached through a hole that passes through the stick from side to side near one end of the stick or the string extends from a hole in the tip of the stick. Most manufactured diabolos come with suitable hand sticks and string. The string is usually about four feet in length.

For safety reasons, I prefer a diabolo with rubber ends. This is not only easier on floors

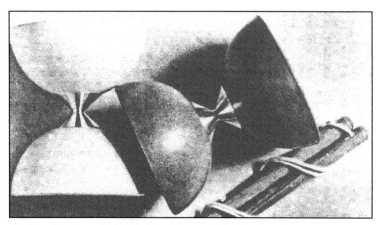

Brian Dube diabolo has machined aluminum center and all rubber ends.

and furniture if used indoors, but also safer if the diabolo should land on you or someone else. I have some all-wood diabolos that are dangerous for anything other than simple basic skills. These are also much more difficult to work than most manufactured plastic and rubber diabolos.

WHAT TO WEAR

No special clothing or protective equipment is required. Most any recreational or leisure attire will do. This should be comfortable and allow freedom of movement.

WORKOUT AREAS

You can practice diabolo skills indoors or outdoors. A reasonably large open area is required. Obviously, you don't want to practice near anything that you can break or damage or trip over. You should also be a safe distance from any other person.

Chapter 4

INDIVIDUAL SKILLS

Diabolo skills are usually mastered in a progressive manner, starting with basic spinning and then building on this. The directions given are for right-handed persons; left-handed persons can reverse directions and hands from the descriptions given. In the descriptions given, the right stick is the power stick.

BASIC SPINNING

The first skill to master is basic spinning. Almost all diabolo tricks begin with basic spinning.

The idea is to start the diabolo spinning on the string and then to keep it spinning and under control, building up spinning revolutions as desired. You already know from our discussion of mechanics that the faster the diabolo is spinning, the more stability it will have.

Begin by placing the diabolo on the floor in front of you about a foot to your right. Stand behind the diabolo and hold the sticks as shown with the string under the diabolo. Roll the diabolo to your left along the floor by lifting upward slightly on the right stick. Then, with the diabolo rolling, quickly bring the right stick upward and move your hands fairly close together. The diabolo should now be spinning a foot or so above the floor.

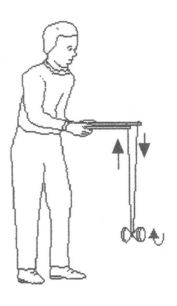

To keep the diabolo spinning, raise the right stick upward rapidly while lowering the left stick just a little. This spins the diabolo in one direction only.

The power stroke is followed by lowering the right stick downward and raising the left stick upward to the starting position, but this time the string is allowed to slip, allowing the top to retain its spin from the power stroke.

By repeating power strokes in this manner, the diabolo can be made to spin faster. The hands and sticks should be close together throughout this action.

The power stroke can be a long smooth stroke or a rapid jerking motion, as desired. In most cases you will want to use the method that gives you the best results.

The axle of the diabolo should be perpendicular to your shoulders. Once the top is spinning rapidly, it tends to stay in the same position. If you find that the diabolo is spinning at an angle to one side, you can move your body position until it is perpendicular to your shoulders.

The spinning diabolo may also tilt towards you or away from you. When the diabolo tilts away from you, bring it back into balance by drawing the right stick in toward you. This should be done while continuing the power strokes.

When the diabolo tilts toward you, bring it back into balance by pushing the right stick away from you while continuing the power strokes.

Important points to keep in mind: The diabolo only spins in one direction, counter-clockwise from the point of view of the performer. Note that if you are standing in front of someone else working the diabolo in the same manner, the diabolo will be spinning clockwise from your point of view.

Only upward motion of the right stick is used to spin the diabolo.

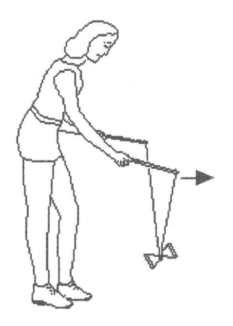

The flat face of the top should be kept parallel to your body. You make corrections by moving your body around to the correct position.

Correction of forward tilt of the diabolo is made by drawing the power stick toward you during the stroking motion. Correction of backward tilt is made by pushing the power stick away from you during the stroking motion.

Many diabolo tricks require the top to be spinning at really high revolutions. Practice until you can build up the speed from slow to high quickly.

TOSS AND CATCH

This trick is also called "Sky Ride." With the diabolo spinning rapidly in basic spinning position, toss it into the air by quickly spreading the sticks apart. A low toss is sufficient on the first attempts, but work up to a toss of at least one foot overhead. Catch the diabolo on the string with the string held tight by spreading the stick apart. The power stick is held higher than the left stick. Sight along the right stick. When the top lands back on the string, bring the sticks quickly together and start the diabolo spinning again.

ROCK

This trick is also called "Swing." With diabolo spinning rapidly, swing it to your right up to shoulder level. Then swing it back down and continue the motion upward to your left up to shoulder level. Return to basic spinning. With practice you can repeat the motion two or more times before returning to basic spinning.

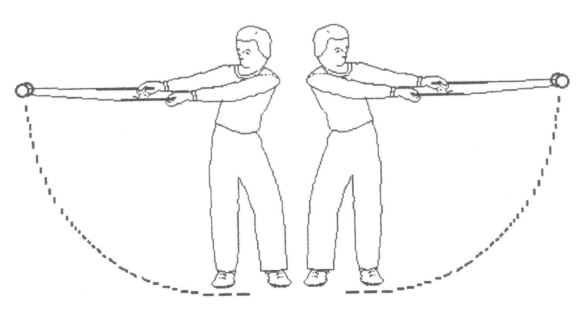

UPHILL CLIMB

This trick is also called "Mountain Climb."

With the diabolo spinning at high speed, lower the right stick so that the top moves to a position near the right stick. Then spread the sticks apart to tighten the string with the right stick lower than the left stick. The top then makes an uphill climb. Finish by returning the sticks to the basic spinning position and resuming normal diabolo spinning.

AROUND THE WORLD

This skill is also called "Windmill," "Giant Circle," and "Rock and Roll." Learn this skill with a lightweight diabolo with rubber ends. A beginner should not attempt this skill with a heavy diabolo that could cause injury should the diabolo strike your head, which is unlikely, but a possibility you will want to avoid.

Begin by building up the diabolo spin to high speed. Then circle your hands and the sticks in front of you to your right. Make a complete circle with the diabolo. The strings will be crossed at the completion of a full circle. Then circle the diabolo back with an Around the World in the opposite direction to the original starting position. The strings will then be uncrossed in the normal spinning position.

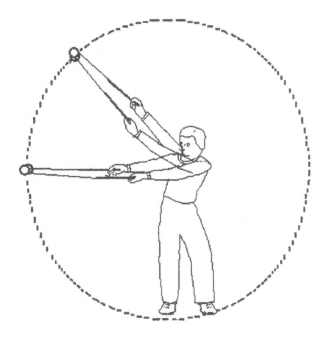

THE WHIP

This is a more advanced method of spinning the diabolo that will give even higher revolutions. This skill is similar to basic spinning, except the diabolo flies from side to side. Your right hand is used to whip the top back and forth in front of you. As the diabolo whips across from your right to left, the right stick crosses behind the string from the left hand stick to the top and under the left elbow. The spinning action is also applied to the diabolo with the right stick as the diabolo is whipped back across.

KANGAROO HOP

This skill is also called "The Walk." Begin with basic spinning. Spread stick outward and overhead, tossing diabolo overhead. Catch diabolo on tight string near tip of right stick. Then let it spin or walk the full length of the string to position near tip of left stick. Flip the diabolo in the air again and catch it near tip of right stick. With practice, the Kangaroo Hop can be repeated four or more times before returning to front spinning position.

STRING BOUNCE

This trick is also called "Cloud Bouncer." Begin with front spinning at high speed. Then toss top overhead. Hold sticks spread apart so that string is tight. Catch diabolo on string so that it bounces on string. Use wrist action to impart bounce, keeping arms overhead. With practice, five or more bounces at least 12 inches in the air can be performed. On the last bounce, bring diabolo back to normal spinning position by relaxing sticks.

BOUNCE BACK

This skill is also called "Touchdown." From basic spinning position, flip diabolo over power stick and allow it to bounce off floor. Catch diabolo back on string and resume basic spinning.

FOOT JUMP

From basic spinning, lower power stick so that diabolo slides to position near power stick. Place your foot on the string above the spinning top and flip top over your foot and catch top on string near left stick. Then repeat flipping diabolo over foot from left to right.

This skill can also be started with diabolo near left stick with this stick lower than the power stick, flipping the diabolo over foot from left to right. The skill can also be done three or more times in succession.

ONE-HANDED SPINNING

This skill is also called "Side Wheeler." From basic spinning, place both sticks in right hand, positioning sticks like open scissors. Spin the diabolo by rocking your right wrist firmly counterclockwise (in direction of diabolo spin) with relaxing action during clockwise rotation to keep diabolo spinning.

One-handed spinning can also be done with both sticks in left hand.

ONE-HANDED TOSS

This skill is also called "Flap Jack." Begin with one-handed spinning with sticks in either hand. Toss diabolo upward. Quickly return sticks to both hands and catch the diabolo on string with regular two-handed position of sticks.

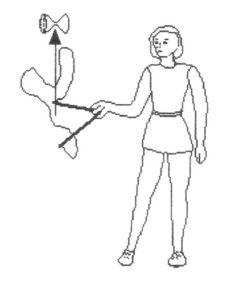

STICK SPIN

From basic spinning position, raise left stick so diabolo spins to position near power stick. Then allow diabolo to roll onto power stick or give diabolo a short toss into air and catch it on power stick, with diabolo still spinning. Balance the spinning top momentarily on stick and then point power stick downward so that the top returns to the string. More difficult is to toss diabolo from power stick and catch it on left stick. Finish by tossing diabolo from left stick and catching it on string.

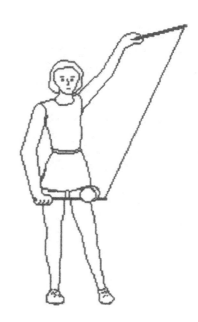

ARM CROSSING

This trick is also called "Cross Toss." Begin with basic spinning. Toss diabolo into air and quickly cross arms. Catch diabolo on tight string. From this position, toss diabolo again and uncross arms. Catch diabolo on string with arms in normal position. More difficult is two or more arm crossings in succession.

JUMPING OVER TOP

This trick is also called "Over the Top." With the top spinning at high speed, lower both sticks so that top is about a foot above the floor. Spread sticks slightly and jump over the top and string. With top still spinning on string behind you, jump backwards over top and string again. Finish with top still spinning on string in front of you.

CROSS STICK CATCH AND TOSS

From basic spinning, toss diabolo a few inches into the air. While diabolo is in air, cross sticks and catch the spinning diabolo in "V" formed by sticks. Allow diabolo to spin in "V" for a few seconds, then toss diabolo into air from sticks and catch it back on string again in normal position.

LOOP

This skill begins the same as the Rock or Swing (detailed previously). As the diabolo swings to your right, place the power stick against the string and allow diabolo to loop the string over the stick. Catch the spinning diabolo on string. Then flip diabolo back to undo loop and resume basic spinning.

DOUBLE LOOP

This one begins with the loop detailed above. With the diabolo spinning on string in loop position swing diabolo under and over power stick again and catch the spinning diabolo on the collected strings. Then with diabolo still spinning, unwind to loop and then again to basic spinning position.

STRING CLIMB

With diabolo spinning rapidly near power stick, loop the power stick forward over the far end of diabolo. With left stick held high, pull down with power stick. The diabolo will then climb up string and pass over left stick to normal string position.

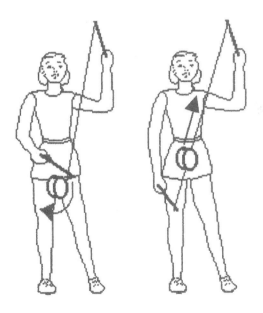

THE CIRCLE CRISSCROSS TOSS AND CATCH

From basic spinning walk around in a circle to opposite side of the diabolo, crossing your arms in route. Then uncross your arms to cross strings, with diabolo still spinning. Then in one quick movement, cross arms again to uncross strings and toss diabolo overhead. Quickly circle back around to original starting position and catch diabolo on string in normal spinning position.

Chapter 5

PARATNER AND GROUP SKILLS

Once you have mastered basic individual diabolo skills, you will want to try partner and group skills. In order to do these skills, each performer should be able to do basic spinning and the Toss and Catch.

CROSS STRING PASS

Begin with two diabolo players side by side. One person does basic spinning. The hand sticks are held so that the strings are tight and crossed, as shown. The diabolo then passes from one string to the next.

This skill can also be performed with a line of three or more players, with the diabolo passed along from one person to the next. In order to pass the diabolo to three or more players, the diabolo must be spinning at rapidly at the start.

TOSS AND CATCH PASS

Tossing the diabolo from one player to another is a fun skill. You will first need to learn the individual toss and catch, as detailed under individual skills. In order to toss the diabolo from one person to another, you must learn to throw accurately. You can toss the diabolo to a person who is standing facing you, back to back, side by side, or front to back. The toss is made with the diabolo spinning rapidly and perfectly balanced. Snap the two hand sticks apart sharply to draw the string tight. The person who catches the diabolo should hold one hand higher than the other. On the first attempts, the power stick is usually higher than the left stick, as shown. Let the center of the diabolo fall on the string as close to the right stick as possible. Then quickly lower the right stick to a position even with the left stick and begin normal spinning action.

Also learn the catch with the left hand stick held higher than the power stick.

More difficult is a catch with an immediate return in combination. To do this, diabolo balance must be maintained after the catch so that an accurate throw can be made. To do this, catch the diabolo in the same direction as it was when tossed to you.

Three or more players can also do toss and catch passing. With a number of players, it is also possible to keep two or more diabolos going at the same time.

The throw, catch, and return are basic skills for playing a diabolo game, as detailed in the next chapter.

Chapter 6

COMPETITION AND GAMES

There are no established rules for diabolo tournaments and games. The following are suggestions.

TOURNAMENTS

Tournaments are usually for individual skills only. If there is a large group of contestants, select a basic skill, such as the Toss and Catch, to be performed by everyone. A miss puts a contestant out of the competition. Those who successfully perform this skill go on to the finals. If there are still too many contestants for the finals, use additional tricks in the same manner.

The finalists then do all of the individual skills detailed in Chapter 4. These are in approximate order of difficulty. A miss on any skill puts a contestant out.

Ties can be settled for those who do all of the skills or the same number of skills by using skills such as the Bounce that can be repeated for record. Another possibility is to perform a series of tricks for time.

COURT DIABOLO

Many diabolo players enjoy informal games, such as tossing the diabolo back and forth to each other long distances. A more formal game that can be played is two or four person court diabolo. Each player needs to be able to do basic spinning

and diabolo balance and the throw, catch, and return, as detailed in previous chapters.

The rules of Court Diabolo are similar to those for badminton or tennis, and the game can be played on a badminton or volley ball court with the net 8 feet high. The diabolo is thrown back and forth over the net. Points are scored when the opposing player drops the diabolo or throws it out of bounds.

Singles

In "Singles" (one person on each side) the "small" court (shown in solid lines in illustration) is used. Each opponent "serves" five consecutive times. Service is made from any point behind the back line and the diabo-

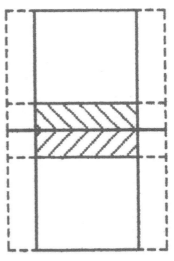

Court for diabolo game.

lo may be tossed over the net into any portion of the opponent's court. The object of the game is to keep the diabolo in motion over the net from court to court without it touching the floor or any portion of the player's body. No player may "hold" the diabolo more than 30 seconds between tosses. Points are scored against the player who fails to catch his opponent's toss or who himself tosses the diabolo out of bounds. The first player to score 50 points is the winner. A foul occurs when a player tosses the diabolo from within the neutral area (shaded in illustration) and a point is scored against him.

Doubles

In "Doubles" (two on each side) the large court (shown in dotted lines on illustration) is used. Each team alternately "serves" five consecutive times. The players on each team alternate service with each team turn—one partner serves 5 times, then on the next team turn the other serves. All other rules are the same as those for "Singles." It is customary in "Doubles" for one player to play at the net, the other deep near the back line.

ABOUT THE AUTHOR

Jack Wiley is the author of fifty published books, including *How to Ride a Unicycle*, *The Complete Book of Unicycling*, *Novelty Unicycling*, *Unicycles and Artistic Bicycles Illustrated*, *How to Build Unicycles and Artistic Bicycles*, *Inside the Wheel: The Complete Guide to Monocycles*, *The Ultimate Wheel Book*, and *On One Wheel: A Unicycling Autobiography*. For more information about the author and his books, go to:

http://www.amazon.com/author/jackwileypublications.

Made in the USA
Monee, IL
04 June 2022

97460667R00020